AF782612

A MONEY MATTERS GUIDE

More for Your Money

a guide to comparison shopping

KEENAN COLTON KELSEY
PATRICIA PARROTT GUNDLACH

GLOBE FEARON

MONEY MATTERS GUIDES

Master Your Money
A Guide to Budgeting

Pay by Check
A Guide to Checking Accounts

More for Your Money
A Guide to Comparison Shopping

Be Ad-Wise
A Guide to Reading Ads

Make Your Money Grow
A Guide to Savings Plans

Insure Yourself
A Guide to Insurance

Be Credit-Wise
A Guide To Credit

Know Your Rights
A Guide to Consumer Protection

PROJECT REVISION TEAM
Editorial Consultant: Stuart E. Schwartz
Content Editor: Craig A. Conley
Executive Editor: Joan Carrafiello
Designer: Pencil Point Studio
Cover Designer: Pencil Point Studio
Production Editor: Rosann Bar
Marketing Manager: Margaret Rakus

Copyright © 1997 by Globe Fearon Educational Publisher, a division of Simon & Schuster, One Lake Street, Upper Saddle River, New Jersey 07458. All rights reserved. No part of this book may be reproduced or transmitted in any form or by any means, electrical or mechanical, including photocopying, recording, or by any information storage and retrieval system except for classroom use, without permission in writing from the publisher.

Printed in the United States of America
1 2 3 4 5 6 7 8 9 10 99 98 97 96

ISBN: 0-8359-3314-8
B-88

GLOBE FEARON EDUCATIONAL PUBLISHER
A Division of Simon & Schuster
Upper Saddle River, New Jersey

Contents

Introduction

This book is about saving money.

After all, no one wants to spend more money than he or she has to. We all want to be smart shoppers.

In this book, you'll read about people who are learning how to save money. They shop for things like clothes, tires, car parts, audio tapes, and food. They know it's important to look closely at different products, different brands, and different stores. That way, they can find the best products and the best prices. They are learning to be smart shoppers by shopping around.

You can learn to compare things when you shop. Then, you too can become a smart shopper.

Now, turn the page and join the fun!

Unit 1 Let's Compare

Jake and Carlos are on their way to basketball practice. They are walking through a shopping center when they see some shirts in a store window.

"Hey, Carlos," Jake says. "Look at this! Wouldn't it be great to show up at the next game wearing shirts that are all alike? We'd look like a real team!"

"Yeah," answers Carlos. "I wonder if everyone would go for the idea. They don't cost much. Let's pick a shirt, then ask the guys."

Look at the shirts in the store window. Then, circle the answer to each question.

1. How many different kinds of shirts are there?

   1 2 3 4

2. Are the sleeves all the same length?

   Yes No

3. Which shirt has no sleeves?

   A B C D

4. Which shirt has short sleeves?

   A B C D

5. Which shirts have long sleeves?

   A B C D

6. Which shirts have stripes?

   A B C D

7. Do the stripes all go in the same direction?

   Yes No

8. Which shirt do you think would be best to wear when you play basketball?

   A B C D

Carlos and Jake compare the shirts and then pick shirt **B,** the one with no sleeves.

When you figure out how things are alike and how they are different, you are comparing things. That's what you did when you answered the questions about the shirts.

Comparing can help you pick things that are best for you.

COMPARING BRANDS

When Jake and Carlos get to the basketball court, Jake notices that Carlos has on new shoes.

"Hey man, new shoes! Great! I got new shoes too. They feel good, but they cost plenty. It took me three weeks to save $45.00."

"45.00!" exclaims Carlos. "I only paid $35.00."

"How can that be?" asks Jake. "Your shoes look just like mine. Why do mine cost more?"

"I see one thing that's different," Carlos tells Jake. "You have *Kelso* brand shoes. They cost a lot. Mine are *People's* brand."

Jake frowns. He remembers a woman at *Mack's Sport Shop* telling him about different brands. She said, "These are *Kelso* shoes. *Kelso* is the company name, or **brand name,** for a certain kind of shoe. Some brands are more expensive than others. But often the expensive brands are better."

Jake is angry at himself for buying the first brand of shoes that he saw. Maybe they are better shoes than Carlos'. But, Jake would rather have the extra dollars in his pocket. He might have saved good money by looking at different brands.

COMPARING BRANDS

The next day, Jake and Carlos see *Kelso* brand shoes in *Dana's Shoe Store*. They are exactly the same as Jake's shoes. But the price is only $42.00.

"You could have saved $3.00!" Carlos says. "You have to shop around in lots of stores."

BE A SMART SHOPPER

Look in the box for the word that belongs in each blank. Then, write in your answer. The first one is done for you.

best
comparing
different
stores
brand

1. You compare things by figuring out how they are alike and how they are ___different___.

2. Comparing can help you pick things that are ________________ for you.

3. A company name for a certain kind of thing is a ________________ name.

4. You can save money by ________________ different brands.

5. You can save money by shopping around in different ________________.

Unit 2 Comparing Products

Have you ever made pizza?

Lynn and George are going to try.

"It'll be fun," says George. "Frozen pizzas just don't cut it. Lynn, if you'll get the tomato sauce and cheese, I'll pick up a pizza pan. I've got everything else we need. Meet me back here around 6:30."

George and Lynn each go off to buy different products. A **product** is anything that is made for sale. The product that George will buy is a pizza pan. What are the two products that Lynn will buy?

____

____

At the store, George finds the pizza pans on a shelf and compares the different kinds. They're all the same size. But George sees that the **contents** are different. One kind is made of aluminum and one kind is made of foil. Even though the foil pans cost less, George picks an aluminum pan. He knows that it will last longer. It is **durable.**

There are lots of ways to compare products. George used four ways to compare the pizza pans:

1. **Size**—Were the sizes of the pans the same or different?

   ____

   The pans were all the *same* size.

2. **Contents** (what the pans are made of)—What were the two kinds of pans made of?

   ____

   ____

   One kind was made of *aluminum.* The other was made of *foil.*

3. **Price**—Which kind costs less?

   ____

   The *foil* pans cost less.

4. **Durability** (how long the pans will last)—Which kind lasts longer?

   ____

   Aluminum pans last longer than foil pans.

MORE WAYS TO COMPARE

Lynn needs to shop for tomato sauce and cheese. Here are two different cans of tomato sauce that she finds in the store.

Lynn compares the sizes and the costs. She sees that the *Delray* sauce is in a bigger can and costs more. What else could Lynn compare on the labels? Circle your answer.

contents   weights   durability

Lynn could compare the **weights** of the sauce inside the cans. Which can has more ounces of tomato sauce in it?

Antioch   Delray

The sauce in the *Delray* can weighs more. But Lynn needs only eight ounces, so she buys the *Antioch.*

Lynn needs cheese for the pizza. She sees that two kinds are grated. So she compares the **number** of cups in each package. Then, she buys the one with three cups.

Look at the packages on page 13. Then put an X on the package with three cups in it.

PUZZLER

Lynn and George used six ways to compare products. Put all six into the puzzle. Here are your clues.

Down

1. How much the products weigh
2. How much the products cost
3. How big the products are
5. What the products are made of

Across

4. How long the products will last
6. How many pieces of the product are in one package

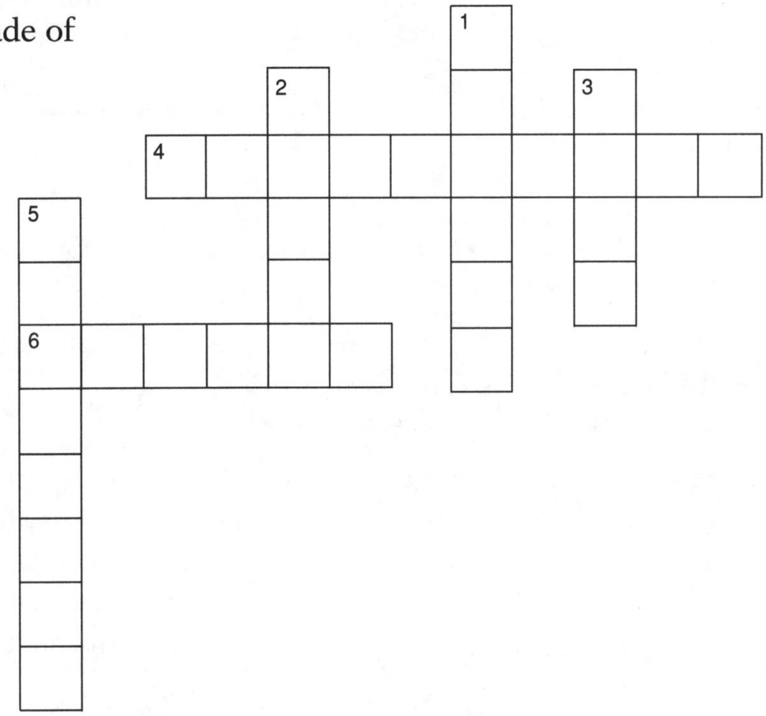

Unit 3 Comparing Stores

Gary and Mike want to tape some music to take along on a trip.

"Hey! Look here," Gary says. "The tapes I just bought cost $1.99. The ones I got last week were only $.99. How can that be?"

Look at the two boxes of tapes in the picture above. Are the brands exactly the same? Circle your answer.

Yes No

Is the playing time the same for both tapes?

Yes No

Do you see any differences in the two boxes?

Yes No

Mike reads the labels. "They're exactly the same brand and have the same playing time. But there are different store names on the price tags. You got these first tapes at *Zacks*. That's the difference. It looks like *Zacks* has a better price than *Melody* has."

Gary and Mike have just learned something important about shopping. Put an **X** by the idea they have learned.

______ Always buy tapes in a music store.

______ The same product will always cost the same amount, even in different stores.

______ The same product might cost different amounts in different stores.

The last answer is right.

Gary tells Mike, "I guess I should have bought more tapes at *Zacks*, since the price is lower. But I wonder if another store has a price even lower than *Zacks* does. Let's see what *Mercury* tapes cost at some other places."

The next day, Gary and Mike each visit another store. They find out the price of *Mercury* tapes with one hour of playing time. Then, they compare all these prices.

A & S Music—$2.05

Crafts—$1.89

Zacks—$1.99

Melody—$.99

Now, compare the four prices by answering these questions.

Is the product the same in each store? ______________________

Is the price the same in each store? ______________________

Which store has the highest price? ______________________

Which store has the lowest price? ______________________

Where do you think Gary should buy tapes? ______________________

MORE COMPARISONS

Gary's friend, Amy, has just bought a used car. It's in good condition, but it has no floor mats. Amy asks Gary what kind she should buy.

"*Riverside* mats are the best," he says. Then, he remembers what happened with his tapes. Gary adds, "Be sure to shop around before you buy."

On her way home from school, Amy goes by the *Auto Club Shop*. The shop sells *Riverside* mats for $45.00 a set.

Next, Amy visits *Liberty Auto Parts*. In that store, *Riverside* floor mats are on sale for $35.00.

This price is much lower than the *Auto Club* price.

That night, Amy looks in the newspaper. She sees an ad for floor mats at the *Auto Clearing House*. The ad lists *Riverside* mats for $39.50.

Now, Amy has three prices to choose from. But she wants to compare them to one more price. She has heard an ad on the radio for *Digit Discounts*. "Shop here for all your needs," the person says. "We have the lowest prices in town."

Digit Discounts is many miles across town. Amy would like to find out the price of *Riverside* floor mats without driving so far. She decides to telephone. The person who answers tells her that the store sells *Riverside* mats for $37.50 a set.

Now, Amy has four prices to choose from. Here are the names of the stores. Write the price of *Riverside* floor mats in each store.

Auto Club Shop $__________

Liberty Auto Parts $__________

Auto Clearing House $__________

Digit Discounts $__________

Where should Amy but her floor mats?

____

Liberty Auto Parts has the lowest price. Amy can get the best buy there.

PUZZLER

Look in the box for the word that belongs in each black. Then, write in your answer.

store
compare
newspaper
buy
telephone
radio
product

1. The same __________________ might cost different amounts in different stores.
2. You can save money by shopping around before you __________________.
3. You can look at the prices in several __________________.
4. You can __________________ stores that are far away.
5. You can read ads in the __________________.
6. You can hear ads on the __________________.
7. It pays to __________________ prices in different stores.

Unit 4

Comparing Packages

Susan, Bill, and Cassie are going with Al to help him buy new tires for his car. They have already compared prices. So, they know that *Anderson's Garage* in a nearby town is the best place to buy tires.

On Saturday morning, they pile into Al's car. But before they start, Bill says, "I'm hungry. And thirsty too. Let's get some things at the supermarket to eat on the way."

PACKAGES WITH THE SAME NUMBER OF ITEMS

At the supermarket, Bill and the others look for small cans of juice. They find that most of them come six to a package. So, it's easy for them to compare prices. They look for the package with the cheapest price.

The friends decide to buy a six-pack of apple juice. On the right, you can see two different six-packs that they compare.

Which six-pack would you choose? Circle your answer.

Sweet Tree Garland's

Why?____________________________________

____

The four friends choose the *Sweet Tree* brand. It costs 40¢ less than the other apple juice. That was easy to figure out because both kinds had the same number of cans in a pack.

Compare the two packages of pens on the right.

How many items are in the package of

Bok pens? ______

How many items are in the *Write-Well*

package? ______

The number is the same for both packages. So, it's easy to compare the prices. Which kind is cheaper? Circle your answer.

Bok Write-Well

The package of *Bok* pens is the better buy.

PACKAGES WITH DIFFERENT NUMBERS OF ITEMS

Different brands of a product don't always have the same number of items in a package. That's what the friends discover when they compare different brands of granola bars. They see two kinds of granola bars.

Cassie says, "Both kinds are good. We should get the kind that cost less."

"Yes," answers Al. "But how can we tell? This box has eight granola bars in it. The other box has twelve. We can't really tell which one is cheaper just by the price of the box."

"No," Susan says. "But we can figure out the price of each *Crunchy* bar and each *Nutty* bar. We should buy the box that costs less for each bar."

THE COST OF EACH ITEM IN A PACKAGE

To find out the cost of each item in a package, you divide the price of the whole package by the number of items in the package.

What is the price of the box of *Crunchy Granola Bars?* $______

The price of the whole box is $2.40.

How many granola bars are in the box of *Crunchy Granola Bars*?______

The number is 8.

To find out the cost of each *Crunchy Granola Bar,* you divide $2.40 by 8. Do the problem below.

8 ⟌ 2.40

In a box of eight *Crunchy Granola Bars,* each bar costs 30¢.

What is the price of the whole box of *Nutty Granola Bars?* $______

The price of the whole box is $4.80.

How many granola bars are in the box of *Nutty Granola Bars?* $______

The number is 12.

To find out the cost of each *Nutty Granola Bar,* you divide $4.80 by 12. Do the problem below.

12 ⟌ 4.80

In a box of 12 *Nutty Granola Bars,* each bar costs 40¢.

Which box costs less for each bar? Circle your answer.

Crunchy Nutty

The friends choose the *Crunchy Granola Bars* because they cost less for each bar in the box.

GETTING A GOOD BUY

Now that the four friends have their juice and granola bars, they drive to *Anderson's Garage.*

While Al is buying his tires, Susan sees a case of 24 cans of motor oil. The price of the whole case is $27.60.

Susan and her friends usually buy one can of oil at a time for $1.69. Could they save money by getting a whole case at a time?

To find out, Susan divides the price of the case by the number of cans in the case. Do the problem below.

$$24\overline{)27.60}$$

The motor oil in the case costs $1.15 a can. That's a lot less than the $1.69 they usually pay.

Susan calls her friends over. "We all have cars," she says. "And we all use motor oil. It costs a lot less to buy the oil by the case. Let's chip in and buy this case together."

Bill, Cassie, and Al agree with Susan. They get a whole case of oil—and a really good buy!

PUZZLE TIME

Look in the box for the word that belongs in each numbered sentence. Then, write that word in the puzzle next to the matching number. The first one is done for you.

package
prices
different
same
number

1. You can get good buys if you compare the ________________ of different packages.

2. You can compare the prices of whole packages when each package has the ________________ number of items.

3. You need to compare the cost of one item in each package when the packages have ________________ numbers of items.

4. To figure out the cost of one item, you divide the price of the whole package by the ________________ of items in the package.

5. The best buy is the ________________ that costs the least for each item in it.

1. p r i c e s
2. _ _ _ e
3. _ _ _ _ _ _ _ e _ _
4. _ _ _ _ e _
5. _ _ _ _ _ _ e

Unit 5

Units of Measure

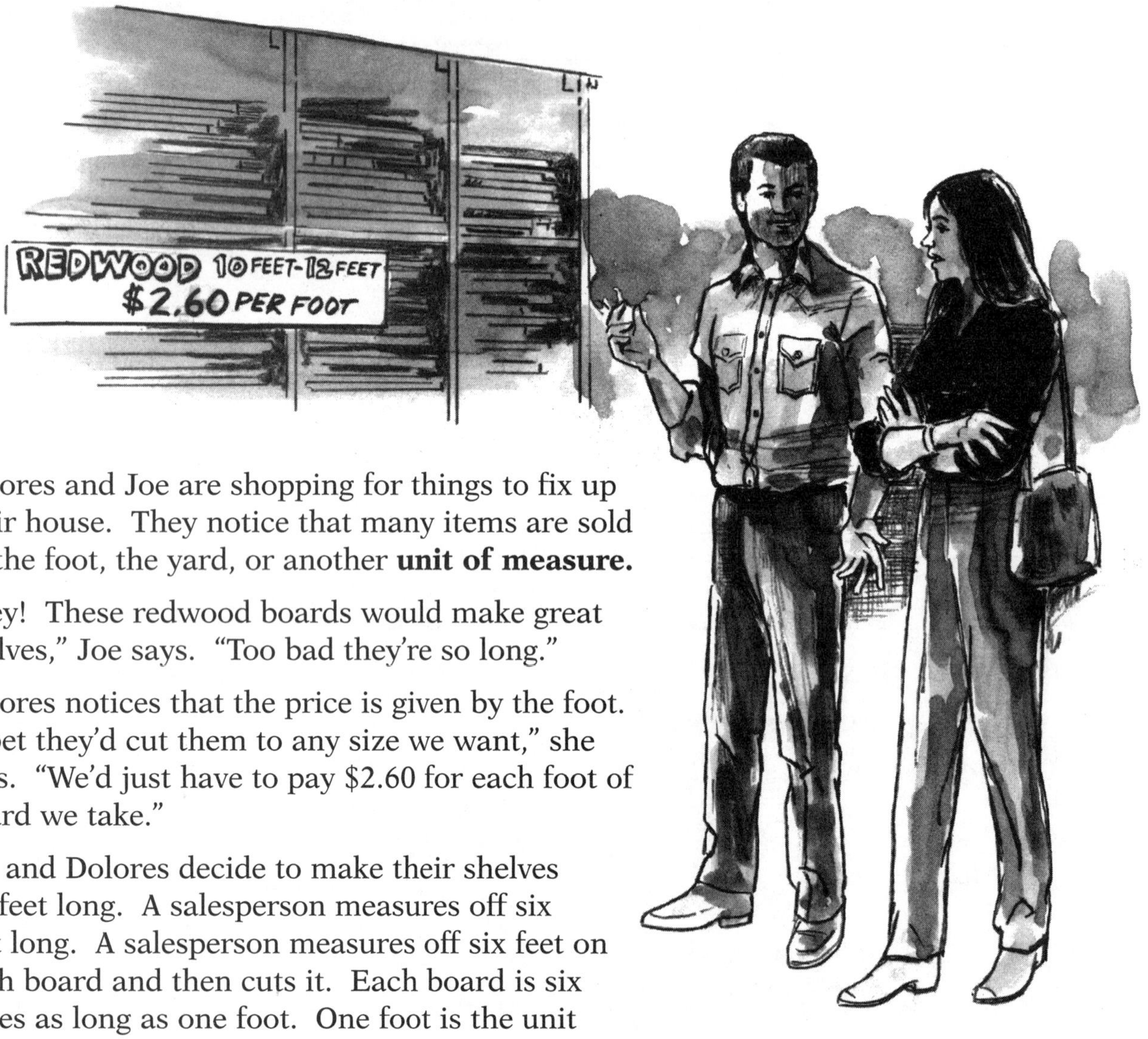

Dolores and Joe are shopping for things to fix up their house. They notice that many items are sold by the foot, the yard, or another **unit of measure.**

"Hey! These redwood boards would make great shelves," Joe says. "Too bad they're so long."

Dolores notices that the price is given by the foot. "I bet they'd cut them to any size we want," she says. "We'd just have to pay $2.60 for each foot of board we take."

Joe and Dolores decide to make their shelves six feet long. A salesperson measures off six feet long. A salesperson measures off six feet on each board and then cuts it. Each board is six times as long as one foot. One foot is the unit used to measure the boards.

"Oh, let's not forget to buy some of that sticky-back shelf paper for the kitchen cabinets," Joe says. "We need about three yards."

They find the shelf paper and ask someone to measure off three yards. The piece of shelf paper that Joe and Dolores buy is three times as long as one yard. What is the unit used to measure the shelf paper?

____

One yard is the unit used to measure the shelf paper.

UNITS FOR MEASURING SIZE

The sizes of different kinds of items in the store are measured in different units. See if you can figure out what the unit of measure is for each item below. Then, circle your answer.

1. **Pine boards**—6 feet, 8 feet, 10 feet

   one foot   one yard   one inch

2. **Shelf paper**—59¢ a yard

   one foot   one yard   one inch

3. **Wrenches**—6 inches, 8 inches, 10 inches, 12 inches

   one foot   one yard   one inch

4. **Ladders**—2 feet, 6 feet, 8 feet

   one foot   one yard   one inch

5. **Screwdrivers**—3 inches, 8 inches, 10 inches

   one foot   one yard   one inch

UNITS FOR MEASURING WEIGHT

Dolores and Joe want to fix part of a cement path that runs along one side of their house.

"Do you think 50 pounds of cement will be enough?" Dolores asks.

"Sure," Joe says. "Only one part needs to be replaced."

They buy the 50-pound bag of cement. How many times heavier is that bag than one pound?

____

It's 50 times as heavy.

What is the unit used to measure the weight of the cement?

____

One pound is the unit of measure.

"While we're working on the house," Joe says, "let's get some concrete cleaner. We can clean the driveway where we park the car. Maybe we can clean the patio, too."

They compare a five-ounce box of concrete cleaner with a 12-ounce container of all-purpose outdoor cleaning powder.

"This concrete cleaner will work on both driveway and the patio," Dolores says. "Let's take the five-ounce box."

They buy the five-ounce box of cleaner. How many times heavier is that box that one ounce?

____

It's five time as heavy.

What is the unit used to measure the weight of the hardener?

____

One ounce is the unit of measure.

UNITS FOR MEASURING CAPACITY

Before leaving the store, Joe and Dolores buy one quart of wood finish to coat a table and chairs. They also buy a two-gallon can of paint for their kitchen and dining room walls.

Wood finish and paint are liquids; they're runny, like water and milk.

To figure out how much liquid you're buying, you need to know how much each bottle or can will hold. The amount of liquid something can hold is its **capacity.**

On the right, there's a picture of the wood finish Joe and Dolores bought.

What is the unit used to measure the capacity of the can of wood finish?

____

One quart is the unit of measure.

Look at the picture of the can of paint Joe and Dolores bought.

What is the unit used to measure the capacity of the can of paint?

____

One gallon is the unit of measure.

How many times one gallon does the can of paint hold?

____

Two times one gallon is the capacity of the can of paint.

UNITS OF MEASURE ON LABELS

When you shop, you want to know how much you're getting for your money. You can find out by looking for the size, weight, or capacity on labels or signs.

Often, you will see the units of measure printed a short way. You will see them abbreviated.

Here are the abbreviations of some units of measure. Look at each abbreviation and read the whole words next to it.

	Abbreviation	Unit
Size	yd.	yard or yards
	ft.	foot or feet
	in.	inch or inches
	m.	meter or meters
	cm.	centimeter or centimeters
	mm.	millimeter or millimeters
Weight	lb.	pound or pounds
	oz.	ounce or ounces
	g.	gram or grams
	kg.	kilogram or kilograms
	mg.	milligram or milligrams
Capacity	gal.	gallon or gallons
	qt.	quart or quarts
	fl. oz.	fluid ounce or fluid ounces
	l.	liter or liters
	ml.	milliliter or milliliters

PUZZLE TIME

The clues to this puzzle use abbreviations for units of measure. On page 28, find the whole word for each abbreviation. Then, use that word to help you complete the crossword puzzle.

Down

1. Joe and Dolores bought two *gal.* of paint.
2. The little girl is one *m.* tall.
4. The car holds 60 *l.* of gasoline.
5. She went to the store to buy a *qt.* of milk.
8. Joe and Dolores bought 50 *lb.* of cement.

Across

3. The medicine bottle is marked off in *ml.*
6. She mailed a letter that weighed just one *oz.*
7. A large bag of potato chips weighs 150 *g.*
9. Redwood boards are sold by the *ft.*
10. The big frying pan is 10 *in.* across.

Unit 6 Comparing Sizes

Sal's sister, Nancy, has just bought some shampoo on sale. It's such a good price that Sal decides to get some for herself.

When she gets back, she goes to Nancy's room. "Look," Sal says. "I saved even more money than you did! This shampoo costs less than yours."

There are pictures of the two bottles of shampoo on the right. Nancy got the *Shining Shampoo.* Sal got the *Jenkins Shampoo.*

Nancy says, "Well, the shampoo you got *does* cost less money. But look at the labels. The bottles don't have the same amount of shampoo in them. The bottle you got holds 14 fluid ounces. My bottle holds 16. You can't tell if you're saving money unless you compare prices for the same amount."

PRICES AND CAPACITY

Sal goes back to the store. This time she looks at the bottles of shampoo very carefully. She sees these different brands.

Look at the capacity marked on each label. What is the unit of measure? Circle your answer.

one yard one fluid ounce one pound

One fluid ounce is the unit of measure.

Two of the bottles hold the same number of fluid ounces.

Circle the pictures of those two bottles.

The bottles of *Shining Shampoo* and *Basic Shampoo* hold the same amount. How many fluid ounces are in each of those two bottles?

____

Each bottle holds 16 fluid ounces.

Now that you are looking at two products that are the same size, it's easy to compare prices.

What is the price of *Shining Shampoo?* $____________

What is the price of *Basic Shampoo?* $____________

Which shampoo costs less?________________________

Nancy made the right choice when she got her shampoo. *Shining Shampoo* does cost less than the other bottle of the same size.

COMPARING OTHER PRICES

While she's at the shore, Sal decides to by some other things. She and her friends are going on a camping trip. Sal is supposed to put together a first-aid kit for the group. She's still missing a few items.

One thing Sal needs is iodine for cuts and bruises. Here are four different bottles that she compares.

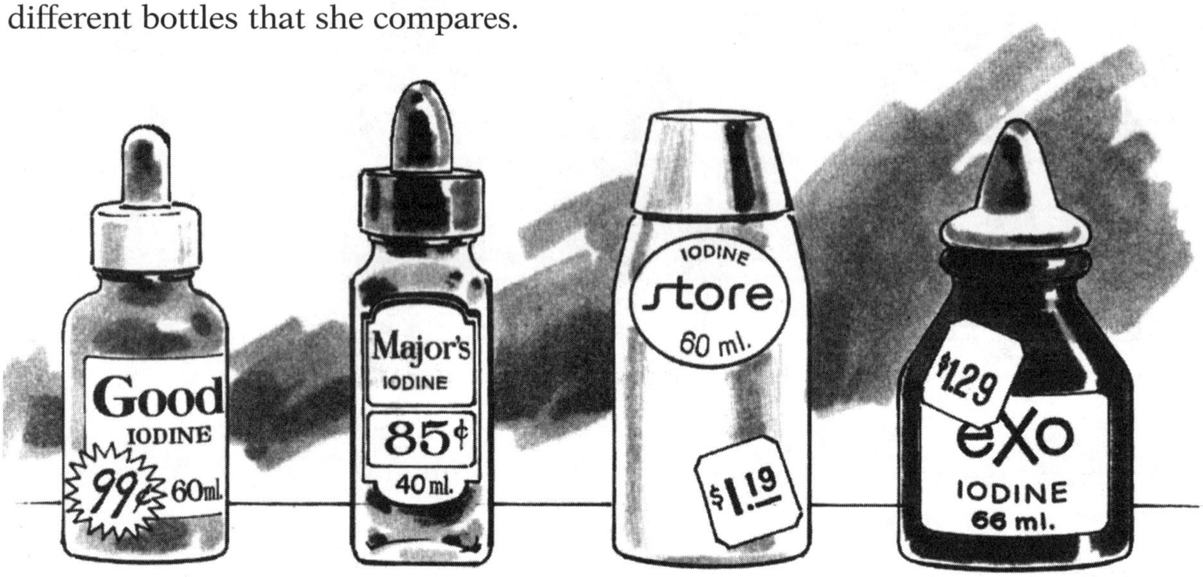

Look at the capacity marked on each label. What is the unit of measure? Circle your answer.

one kilogram   one foot   one milliliter

One milliliter is the unit of measure.

Two of the bottles hold the same number of milliliters. Circle the pictures of those two bottles.

The bottles of *Good Iodine* and *Store Iodine* hold the same amount.

How many milliliters are in each of those two bottles? __________

Each bottle holds 60 milliliters.

Which of those two bottles cost less?

____

Good Iodine costs less. Sal buys that brand for the first-aid kit.

PRICES AND SIZES

A first-aid kit needs a long, elastic bandage in case of sprained ankles or arms. Sal finds four different bandages. They're all the same length, but the widths are different.

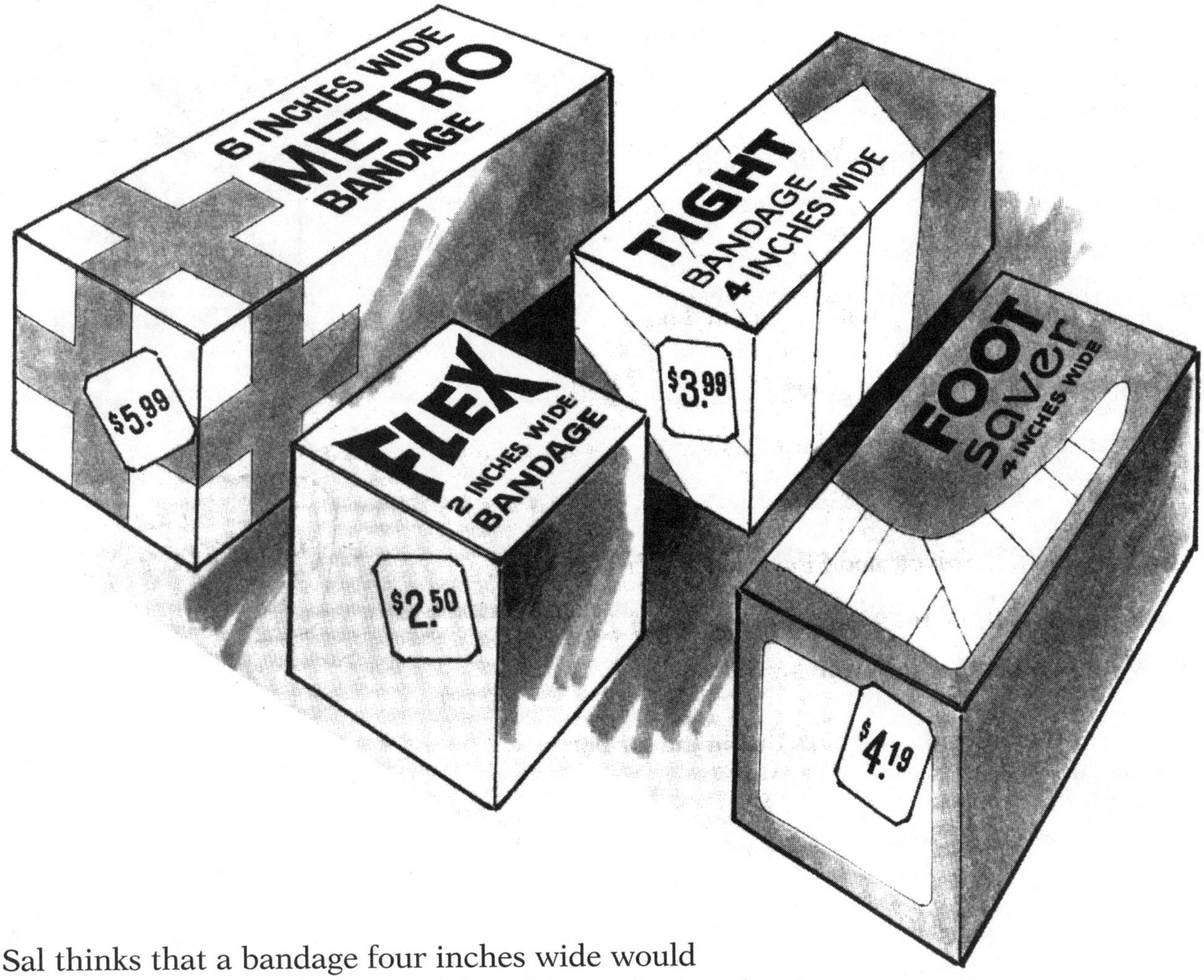

Sal thinks that a bandage four inches wide would be a good size. Which four-inch bandage is the best buy?

____

Tight Bandage costs less than the other four-inch bandage. Sal decides to get the *Tight Bandage* for the kit.

PRICES AND WEIGHT

When Sal bought the shampoo, she made a mistake. She did not look at the size of each bottle. Sal was fooled by the different shapes of the bottles.

Sal has learned to look at the sizes of products more carefully. When she shops for her first-aid kit, she makes sure that she compares prices on the same amount of each product.

The last thing that Sal needs to buy for the kit is petroleum jelly for dry and chapped skin. She sees the jars pictured at the right.

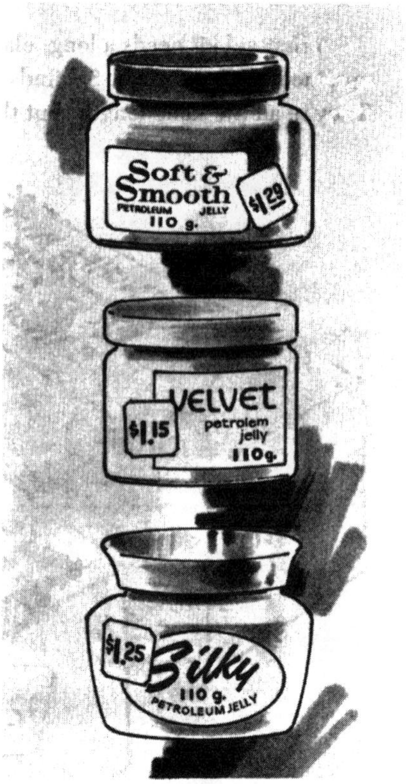

What is the unit of measure for each jar? Circle your answer.

one quart   one gram   one meter

One gram is the unit of measure.

How heavy is each of those three jars?

110 grams   220 grams   200 grams

Soft & Smooth, Velvet, and *Silky* each weigh 110 grams.

Which one of those three jars costs the least?

Soft & Smooth   Velvet   Silky

Velvet is the best buy. Sal buys that brand for her first-aid kit.

PUZZLE TIME

Each puzzle clue lists three brands of a product. Compare the sizes and prices. Then, circle the brand name of the product that's the best buy. The correct answers are hidden in the puzzle. Find and circle each answer. The brand names are printed across, down, up, and on a slant. The first one is done for you.

1. Tubes of toothpaste

Best	Gorgeous	Shine
6.5 oz.	4 oz.	6.5 oz.
89¢	89¢	85¢

2. Bottles of milk

Farmland	Tasty	Parsons
1 qt.	1 qt.	1/2 gal.
49¢	51¢	$1.00

3. Boneless hams

Bar-B	Hilltop	Simon's
$2.29 a lb.	$2.09 a lb.	$2.19 a lb.

4. Bottles of cold medicine

Breathe	Fresh Air	Sneeze Gone
10 fl. oz.	8 fl. oz.	10 fl. oz.
$3.79	$3.79	$3.89

5. Rolls of aluminum foil

Wrap-All	Finest	Super
75-ft. roll	50-ft. roll	75-ft. roll
$1.39	$1.29	$1.29

A	B	C	D	E	F	B	G	H
I	J	K	L	M	N	R	O	P
Q	R	S	T	U	V	E	W	R
X	S	Y	Z	A	B	A	C	E
D	E	H	I	L	L	T	O	P
F	G	H	I	I	J	H	K	U
L	M	N	O	N	E	E	P	S
Q	R	S	T	U	E	V	W	X
F	A	R	M	L	A	N	D	Y

Unit 7 Finding Prices per Unit

Raymond and Marcy are having a party.

They already have most of the things they need. "But not everything," says Marcy. "We still need the ground turkey. We could use some pickles, and we need ice cream for dessert."

Raymond frowns. He counts their money. "We only have $10.00 left. Can we get all that?"

"We'll just get as much as we can," answers Marcy. "But if we shop carefully, I think we can get everything. Let's go see."

At the store, the two friends start with the meat. They find ground turkey in a two-pound package for $4.20. They also see ground turkey in a three-pound package for $5.70.

Which package has the lower price? Circle your answer.

two-pound three-pounder

The two-pound package costs less. Would Marcy and Raymond save money by getting that package?

Yes No Can't tell

"I guess we could use three pounds of meat," Marcy says. "But we can't tell if we're saving money unless we compare prices for the same amount of meat."

"We can figure out the cost of each pound of meat in the two-pound package," Raymond says. "Then we can figure out the cost of each pound of meat in the three-pound package. We should buy the package that costs less **per** pound."

Per pound means *for* each pound. Raymond and Marcy will buy the package that costs less for each pound.

Whenever you want to compare the prices of packages with different numbers of units, you can figure out the cost per unit. Then, you can compare the cost for one unit in one package with the cost for one unit in other packages.

FINDING THE COST PER UNIT

To find out the cost of each unit in a package, you divide the price of the whole package by the number of units in the package.

In the picture above, you can see the packages of meat that Raymond and Marcy want to compare.

What is the price of the two-pound package of meat? $__________

The price of the package is $4.20.

The unit of measure is one pound. How many units are in the two-pound package?

____

The number is 2.

To find out the cost of each unit, you divide $4.20 by 2. Do the problem below.

$2\overline{)\,4.20}$

In the two-pound package, the cost of the meat is $2.10 per pound.

What is the price of the three-pound package of meat? __________

The price is $5.70.

How many units are in the three-pound package? __________

The number is 3.

To find out the cost per pound of meat in the larger package, you divide $5.70 by 3. Do the problem below.

$3\overline{)\,5.70}$

In the three-pound package, the meat costs $1.90 per pound.

Which package of meat costs less per pound? Circle your answer.

two-pound package three-pound package

Raymond and Marcy choose the three-pound package. It costs less per pound of meat. And they know they can use three pounds.

FINDING THE COST PER OUNCE

Next, Raymond and Marcy look for pickles. They find the brands shown below.

Which brand costs less per ounce? To find out, Raymond and Marcy divide the price of each jar by the number of ounces in that jar.

How much do *Piper Pickles* cost per ounce? To find out, do problem number 1 at the right.

1. $20\overline{)1.00}$

Piper Pickles cost 5¢ per ounce.

How much co *Lutz Pickles* cost per ounce? To find out, do problem number 2 at the right.

2. $24\overline{)1.44}$

Lutz Pickles cost 6¢ per ounce.

Raymond and Marcy buy the cheaper brand. Which kind do they buy?

Piper Pickles　　　Lutz Pickles.

They buy the *Piper Pickles.*

ADDING IT UP

Ice cream is the last thing on Raymond and Marcy's shopping list.

"There's only one kind here that I really like," says Marcy. "Aunt Elsie's. It's $3.20 for a half gallon. Do we have enough money left?"

"Let's see," Raymond answers. "We're getting the ground turkey for $5.70 and the pickles for $1.00."

What is their total so far? Add up the amounts below.

$$\begin{array}{r} \$\,5.70 \\ +\;\;1.00 \\ \hline \$ \end{array}$$

"That's $6.70 so far," Marcy says.

Raymond and Marcy started out with $10.00. After they subtract the $6.70, how much will be left for ice cream? Do the problem below.

$$\begin{array}{r} \$\,10.00 \\ -\;\;6.70 \\ \hline \$ \end{array}$$

They'll have $3.30 left for ice cream. The kind they want costs $3.20.

"We made it!" Raymond says. "It sure pays to compare prices."

PUZZLE TIME

Look in the box for the word that belongs in each sentence clue. Then write in your answer. Use your answers to complete the crossword puzzle.

same
per
unit
each
price
product

Down

1. The cost *per* unit means the cost for ______________ unit.

2. To compare the prices of packages with different numbers of units, you need to figure out the cost ______________ unit.

3. When you compare the costs for one ______________ in each of several packages, you are comparing costs for the same amount of a product.

Across

2. You can save money by buying the ______________ that costs the least per unit.

4. You can't tell if you're saving money unless you compare prices for the ______________ amount of a product.

5. To find the cost of each unit in a package, you divide the ______________ of the whole package by the number of units in the package.

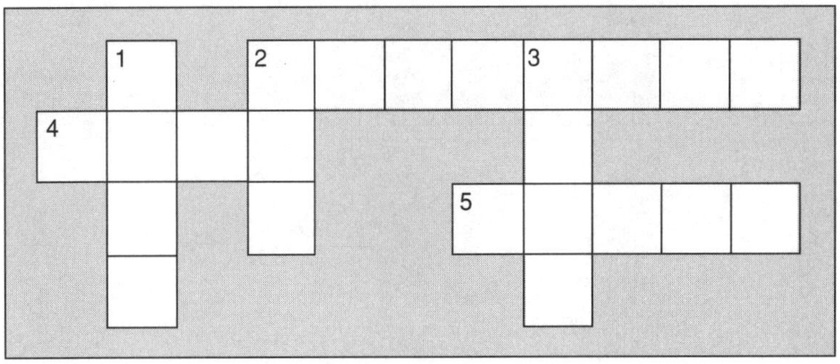

REVIEW TIME

Read each sentence below. Then decide if the sentence is true or false. If it's true, write a **T** on the line. If it's false, write an **F**.

______ **1.** You can save money by shopping at different stores.

______ **2.** Comparing products helps you pick what's best for you.

______ **3.** All brands of a product are the same price.

Suppose you wanted ten cans of *Super Bounce* tennis balls. How could you get the best buy? Circle each sentence that gives a good idea.

1. Go to any store and buy the tennis balls without shopping around.

2. Check the prices at several stores.

3. Look for ads in the newspaper, and listen to ads on the radio.

Match each unit of measure with its abbreviation. Draw a line from the whole word to the short form. If you need help, turn to page 28. The first one is done for you.

1. inch	oz
2. gram	lb.
3. ounce	in.
4. quart	qt.
5. foot	g.
6. pound	ft.

Look in the box for the word that belongs in each blank. Then write in your answer.

each
item
compare
units
different
same

1. To get good buys, you need to _______________ the prices of different packages.

2. It's easy to compare the prices of whole packages. But all the packages must have the _______________ number of items or units.

3. Some packages have _______________ numbers of items or units. Then, you need to compare the costs per item or per units.

4. The cost *per* item or unit means the cost for _______________ item or unit.

5. You can find the cost of each item or unit in a package. Just divide the price of the whole package by the number of items or _______________ in the package.

6. You can save money by buying the product that costs the least per _______________ or unit.

Unit 8 Quality Counts Too

You have been comparing the prices of products in different stores and in packages of different sizes. But price isn't the only thing that's important. When you shop, you'll also want to think about the **quality** of the products you buy.

When you decide how good products are, you are judging the quality of those products.

How can you judge the quality of products? To decide how good products are, you'll want to see how well they're made and what they're made of. The things that products are made of are the **contents** of those products.

Anna wants to buy a warm jacket. She and May compare the quality of different jackets. Anna holds up a brown one. "Now, this is really nice. But it's so expensive."

May brings over some more jackets. "Do you like any of these?"

Anna finds three jackets in the right color and size. "Look at these prices!" she says. "They're all different."

May touches the outside of each jacket and the inside of the one that's lined. "The jackets feel different too," she says. "Let's see what they're made of."

Anna looks at the list of contents shown at the top of each price tag. Here's what she finds.

All-Wool Rayon Lining Size 8 $65.00	All-Wool Size 8 $55.00	Wool and Dacron Size 8 $49.00

"Well," May says. "Now we know why the prices are different."

Why are the prices different? Do all the jackets have linings? Circle your answer.

Yes No

No. Only the $65.00 jacket is lined. That's one reason why it costs more than the other two jackets.

Are all three jackets made out of the same material?

Yes No

No. Two of the jackets are all-wool. The $49.00 jacket is made of wool and dacron.

May says, "Things that are all-wool are usually warmer than things made out of wool mixed with other materials. Maybe that's why the wool and dacron jacket costs less than the other two."

Anna tries on each of the jackets. "The all-wool jackets *do* seem warmer," she says. "I think they're worth some extra money. But I'm not sure, I really need the lining."

May looks at the way the jackets are sewn. She sees that the $55.00 jacket is made very well.

Then she lifts the lining of the most expensive jacket. "This sewing is very sloppy," May says. "The lining hides the poor quality. It's not really worth more than the other wool jacket."

Which jacket do you think Anna should buy? Circle the price that shows your answer.

$65.00 $55.00 $49.00

Why did you choose that answer?

____

____

____

Anna decides to get the $55.00 jacket. It's all-wool, so it's warm. And the jacket is made well. The quality of the contents and the sewing is very good.

COMPARING THE QUALITY OF FOODS

On the way home from the store, Anna begins to feel hungry, "I'm starved, May. Do you have anything to eat at your place?"

"Not much," answers May. "Just bread and milk. But if we stop and get some ham spread, we can make sandwiches."

At the supermarket, they find two brands of ham spread. "Why does one brand costs so much more than the other one?" Anna asks.

May says, "Maybe they're not made out of the same things. Look at the lists of ingredients."

The things that food products are made of are the **ingredients** of those products.

Look at the pictures of the two cans of ham spread. On each label, put a large **X** next to the list of ingredients.

Ingredients are listed in a certain order. The first one in the list is the main ingredient. There is more of that ingredient in the product than there is of any other ingredient.

What is the main ingredient in *Ham Delight?* Circle your answer.

Pork fat   Ham   Water   Onion

Ham is the main ingredient in *Ham Delight.*

What is the main ingredient in *Deviled Ham Spread?*

Pork fat   Ham   Water   Onion

Pork fat is the answer.

Which brand is better in quality?

Ham Delight   Deviled Ham Spread

Why did you choose that answer?

____

____

May says, "I don't want to eat a spread that has so much fat in it. I'd rather pay the extra money for the better ingredients. Let's get the *Ham Delight.*"

IT'S UP TO YOU

Anna and May chose the ham spread that was higher in quality—the one with better ingredients. It was also the ham spread with the higher price.

Which ham spread would you choose?

The answer depends on what's important to you when you shop for food. Sometimes the price might be more important to you than the quality. Or you might care more about the taste than the ingredients.

What's most important to you when you shop for clothes? Circle your answer.

- **a.** Appearance
- **b.** Price
- **c.** How they must be cleaned—washed by hand, washed in a machine, or dry cleaned
- **d.** Quality—how they're made and what they're made of

Suppose you were shopping for a car. What would be most important to you?

- **a.** Appearance
- **b.** Price
- **c.** Quality—safety, well-made engine and other parts
- **d.** Gas mileage

There are no right or wrong answers to these questions. The important thing is to know everything about the products you're comparing. Then, you can decide which product is best for you.

PUZZLE TIME

Here are eight words that smart shoppers use. But the letters in each word are all mixed up. Use the clue under each word to help you unscramble the letters. Then, write the word on the line.

If you need an extra clue, look at the words in the box. The first one is done for you.

contents
safety
price
compares
quality
brands
appearance
ingredients

1. e r c i p ___price___
The cost of a product

2. a i u y t l q ______________
How well a product is made

3. t t s n n c o e ______________
What a product is made of

4. g r e d i n i e n t s ______________
Another word for contents

5. a e a a e p p r n c ______________
How something looks

6. t y e f a s ______________
How safe a product is

7. d r a n b s ______________
Names of products from different companies

8. p a r e c o m s ______________
What a smart shopper does

Unit 9 How Long Will It Last?

Have you ever heard someone on TV tell you that a product will last a long time? You might hear something like this: "Our furniture is beautiful, the price is right, and it wears like iron! It will last you a lifetime."

The commercial may or may not be true. But some products *do* last longer than others. We say that something that lasts a long time is **durable.** When we talk about the *durability* of a product, we discuss the length of time the product will last.

JUDGING DURABILITY

When you are looking for a good buy, it can help to think about a product's durability.

Here are four sets of products. Circle the one in each set that you think will last longer.

The hardcover book will hold together longer than the paperback.

The strong clog shoes will wear longer than the sandals.

The thick sponge will last longer than the thin one.

The better-made shirt will not tear as soon as the other one.

DURABILITY AND PRICE

Items with greater durability will often cost more. When you go shopping, it is up to you to decide if you want to spend extra money for something that will last a longer time.

Kim must decide about durability when she shops for car batteries.

Kim goes to the *Car Discount Center.* A salesperson shows her three kinds of batteries.

"Each of these batteries will last a different length of time," the salesperson explains.

"This *Royal* battery costs only $40.00. And, it will last for three years."

"The *Norris* battery costs more. It's $68.00, but it will last for five years.

"The most expensive battery is the *Superking* brand. It costs $100.00, but it will last as long as you own your car. If it ever breaks down, we will give you a new one free."

Kim plans to trade in her car in about two years. Which battery do you think she will buy now? Circle your answer.

Royal Norris Superking

Kim picks the least expensive one, the *Royal* battery. She does not need one that lasts a long time.

Kim's brother is fixing up a car he bought. He plans to keep the car for five or six years. Which kind of battery do you think he will buy?

Royal Norris Superking

Kim's brother buys the *Norris* battery. It will last as long as he plans to own his car. There's no need for him to spend more money on the most expensive battery.

Kim's grandmother also needs a new battery for her car. She owns a very expensive car. She wants to keep it for at least ten years. Which battery do you think she will buy?

Royal Norris Superking

The *Superking* battery is the only kind durable enough for Kim's grandmother. If she gets a cheaper kind, she'll have to replace it before she's ready to sell her car. She saves money by getting the most expensive kind.

CHOOSING A PRODUCT BY DURABILITY

Different kinds of products are shown on these two pages. Different people are also described.

Think about the length of time each product might last. Then, think about each person's needs. Decide which product would be best for each person.

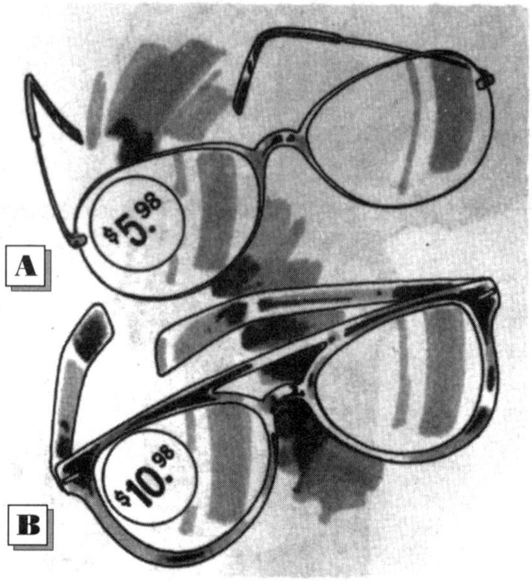

Bonnie wears sunglasses all the time. But she also loses them all the time. She can't keep one pair longer than a week. Which pair do you think she should buy,

A or **B**? ______

Ben wears sunglasses a lot too. He's always dropping them. So, he doesn't want ones that will break easily. Which pair do you think he should buy? ______

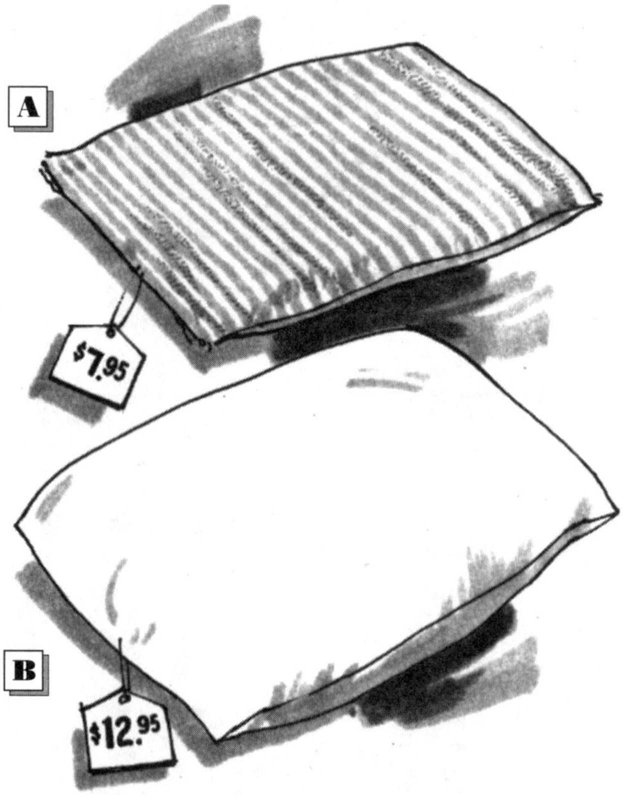

Angel sleeps with her pillow crushed in her arms. It takes Angel weeks to get a pillow just the way she likes it. She doesn't want to break in a new pillow every few months. Which pillow do you think she should buy? ______

Andrew also needs a new pillow. But he usually pushes his pillow onto the floor. Which one do you think he should buy? _____

Bill is using an old pickup truck that he will drive for one summer. It needs new tires.

Which tires do you think he should buy? **A** or **B**? ______

Carmen's car also needs new tires. But she uses her car every day to make deliveries for a flower shop. Which tires do you think she should buy? ______

Edith is learning how to play baseball. She can hit the ball just fine, but she needs practice catching and fielding the ball. Her friend Sid throws with her sometimes on weekends. Which baseball glove do you think she should buy? ______

Sid is already a good baseball player. He is on a team that plays twice a week. When he needs a new glove, which one do you think he should buy? ______

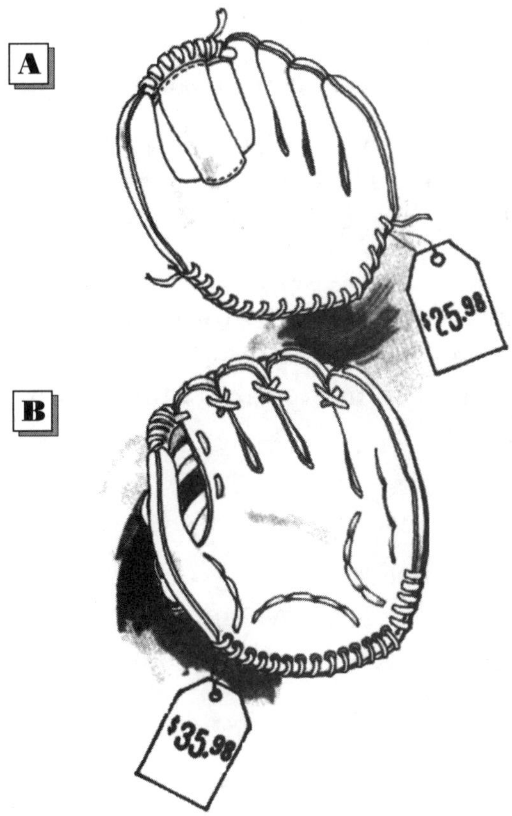

Unit 10 Six Ways to Compare

Getting the most for your money—it isn't quite as easy as you thought, is it?

When you shop, you need to compare products to see all the ways that they are alike and different. Then, you can pick the ones that are best for you.

You'll want to find the lowest prices when you shop. To do that, you need to compare different brands of products in different stores. And, sometimes you need to figure out the price per item or the price per unit of measure in a package.

You'll want to buy the size or amount of a product that's right for your needs.

To get the best buy, you will also want to compare the quality of the contents or ingredients of products.

You'll want to see how well the products are put together. That will tell you something about their durability. Products last longer when they are made well.

There are many things to think about when you shop. But you *can* be a good comparison shopper. Just remember to compare the six things at the right.

1. Products
2. Stores
3. Sizes
4. Prices
5. Contents
6. Durability

PUZZLER

Look at the list on page 56 for the word that belongs in each sentence clue. Then write in your answer. Use your answers to complete the crossword puzzle.

Across

1. You compare _______________ to see all the ways that they are alike and different.

5. You compare _______________ to make sure you get the right amount.

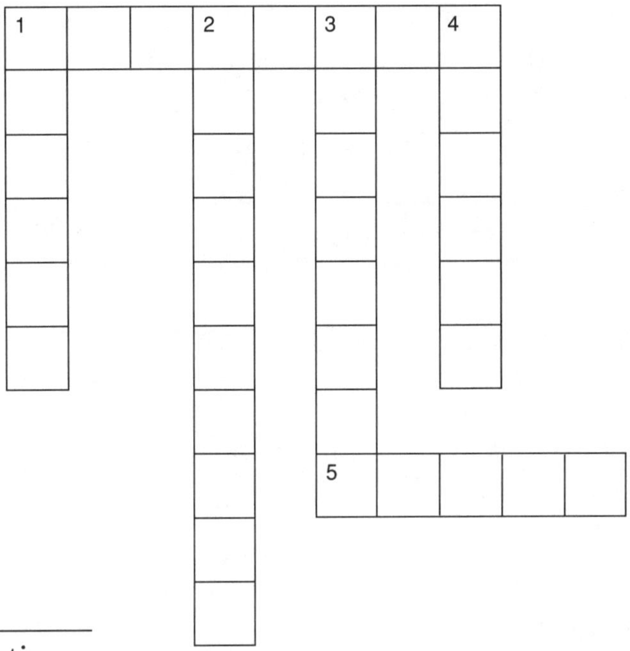

Down

1. You compare the _______________ to find the lowest ones.

2. When you compare the _______________ of products, you judge the length of time they will last.

3. You need to compare the quality of the _______________ or ingredients of products.

4. You need to compare the prices of products in different _______________.

On the next few pages, you will read about people with shopping problems. As you help them decide what to buy, you will help yourself become a smart shopper.

Denise has four plants that are growing quickly. She needs to buy larger flowerpots for them.

COMPARING PRODUCTS

Denise does not want to spend a lot of money for fancy, expensive flowerpots.

Compare the two pots shown at the bottom of the page. Circle the kind you think Denise should shop for.

COMPARING STORES

Denise looks at plain flowerpots in several stores. She finds the prices listed below.

Circle the name of the store where she might get the best buy.

Havens Hardware Store	Romans Department Store	Indoor Garden Shop
$3.49	$3.69	$3.29

The *Indoor Garden Shop* seems to have the lowest price for the kind of flowerpot Denise wants.

COMPARING SIZES

All of Denise's plants are not in 6-inch pots. She needs larger pots. Which size would be big enough? Circle your answer.

2-inch pots 4-inch pots 10-inch pots

Denise needs 10-inch pots now.

COMPARING CONTENTS AND DURABILITY

Here are two kinds of pots that Denise sees.

Denise has a cat that jumps on her furniture and knocks over her plants. She knows that clay pots break easily. The plastic pots will not break so easily. Do you think that Denise should pay extra for plastic pots?

Yes No

Denise decides to buy the plastic pots so that they will last longer.

COMPARING PRICES

Denise sees two different brands of plastic flowerpots. One brand costs $3.50 per pot. The other brand comes in a package of four pots for $15.20.

Denise needs to find out which brand costs less per pot. She divides the price of the package by the number of pots in the package. Do the problem below.

$$4 \overline{)15.20}$$

The packaged flowerpots cost $3.80 per pot. Denise buys four of the $3.50 pots.

Jackson has a new dog. He knows that the puppy will eat a lot as it grows up. Jackson wants to be sure that he finds the best dog food. But he wants to get a good buy on that food.

COMPARING PRODUCTS

Dog food comes in cans and in bags. The cans hold single servings, but the bags of dry food hold many servings. The smallest bag of dry dog food is five pounds. Jackson has very little extra space to store things. Should he buy the smaller cans or the larger bags?

____

Jackson decides that he does not have room to store bags of dog food. He will buy the product in the small cans.

COMPARING STORES

Jackson compares the prices for canned dog food in two stores, a pet shop, and a supermarket.

The pet shop sells only one brand for 65¢ a can.

The supermarket sells many brands. The lowest price is 32¢ a can. The highest price is 60¢ a can.

Where do you think Jackson will get the best buy? Circle your answer.

Pet shop   Supermarket

Jackson decides to shop at the supermarket.

COMPARING SIZES

At the supermarket, Jackson compares the three brands of dog food shown on page 61.

Do all the cans have the same amount of dog food in them?

Yes   No

No. The cans *look* as if they're the same size. But their weights are different. It pays to look closely at labels.

COMPARING PRICES

Which of the three brands costs the least per ounce? To find out, divide the price of each can by the number of ounces in that can. Do the problem below.

Bowser	Super Dog	Temple
$13\overline{)\,.52}$	$14\overline{)\,.42}$	$15\overline{)\,.60}$

Bowser and *Temple* each cost 4¢ per ounce. *Super Dog* costs only 3¢ per ounce.

COMPARING CONTENTS AND DURABILITY

Durability is not important when you compare dog foods.

But the contents *are* important. Each brand is made of different ingredients. Remember that the main ingredient is always listed first.

What is the main ingredient in *Bowser?*

____

What is the main ingredient in *Super Dog?*

____

What is the main ingredient in *Temple?*

____

Bowser is made mostly of meat by-products. *Super Dog* is made mostly of water. *Temple* is made mostly of meat. Jackson knows that a dog needs meat and vitamins to grow strong. He decides to pay a little more per ounce. He buys the *Temple* dog food.

Suppose you were shopping for a hammer, and you saw all these different kinds.

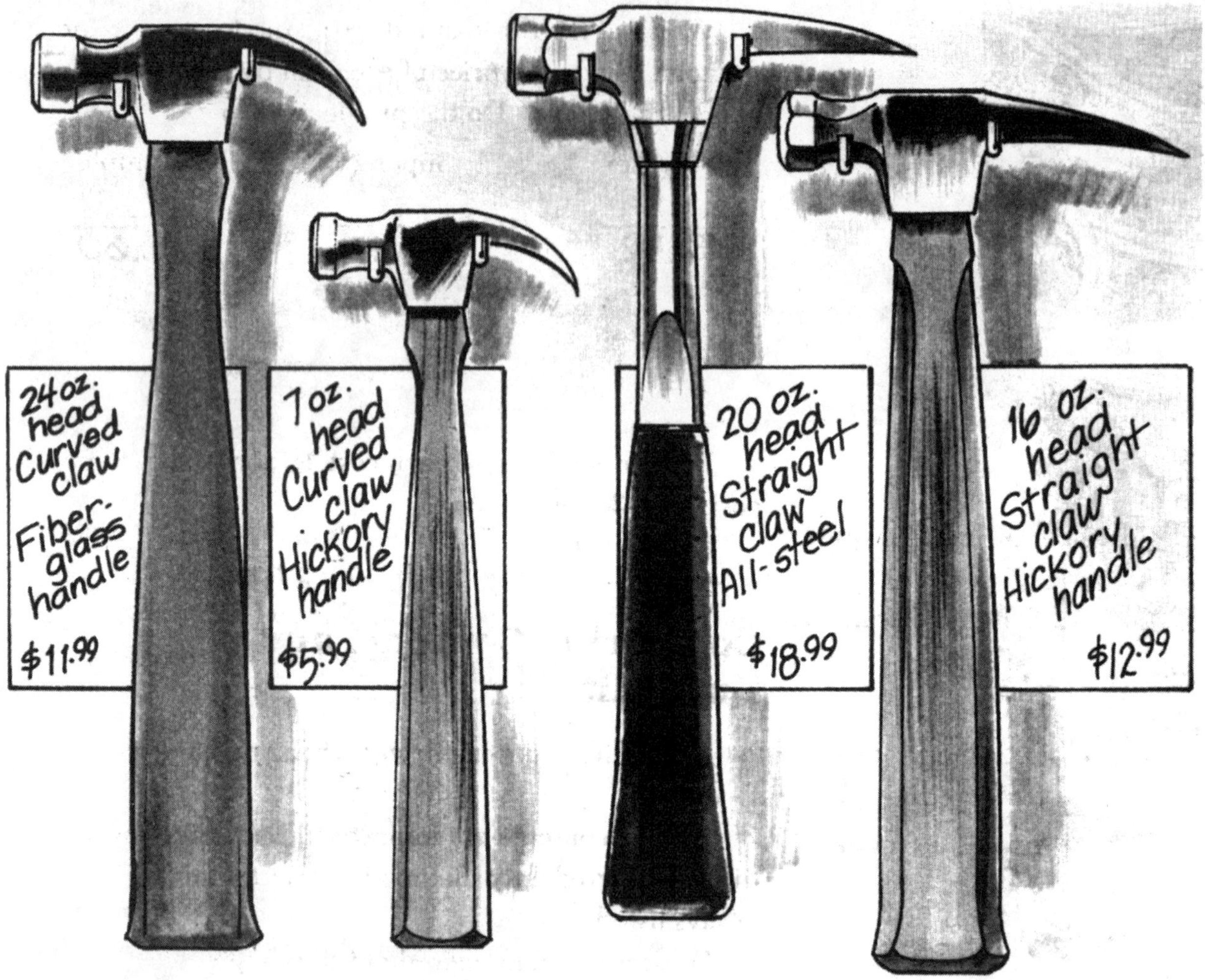

COMPARING PRODUCTS

Which two hammers have curved claws at the top? Circle your answers.

A B C D

COMPARING CONTENTS

Which two hammers have hickory handles?

A B C D

Which hammer is all-steel?

A B C D

COMPARING SIZES

Which hammer has the heaviest head?

A B C D

COMPARING PRICES

Which hammer costs the most?

A B C D

COMPARING DURABILITY

Why do you think the all-steel hammer costs the most?

____

____

Steel is very strong. Hammer C will probably last the longest.

You have just compared the hammers in five different ways. But to get the best buy, you need to do one more thing. What is it?

____

____

You need to compare the prices of hammers in different stores.

Whenever you shop for an expensive item, you might want to fill out a copy of this Shopper's Guide.

Shopper's Guide

Kind of product (bike, TV, etc.) ______________________________

Brand names				
Sizes				
Contents or Ingredients				
Durability				
Prices				
My choice (Check one.)				

Stores where my choice is sold				
Prices				
Best buy (Check one.)				

Copy Master. Globe Fearon Publishers hereby grants permission to readers of this book to make copies of the Shopper's Guide for their use only.